I0055546

MASTERING THE POWER OF COMMUNICATION

Book 5

8 Books to 8 Figures Series

JASON MILLER

Copyright 2024 Jason Miller

ALL RIGHTS RESERVED. This book contains material protected under International and Federal Copyright Laws and Treaties. Any un-authorized reprint or use of this material is prohibited. No part of this book may be reproduced or transmitted in any form or by any means, electronic or mechanical, including photocopying, recording, or by any information storage and retrieval system, without express written permission from the author/publisher.

ISBN: 978-1-957217-51-2 (hardcover)
ISBN: 978-1-957217-52-9 (paperback)
ISBN: 978-1-957217-53-6 (ebook)

TABLE OF CONTENTS

INTRODUCTION

Communication is the lifeblood of any business. It's how we connect, share ideas, and get things done. But what exactly is communication? Well, it's more than just talking or sending emails. Communication is about conveying information, whether it's through words, gestures, or even facial expressions. It's the exchange of thoughts, ideas, and messages between people or groups.

In business, effective communication is crucial. It keeps our teams aligned, our customers satisfied, and our operations running smoothly. Without clear communication, tasks can get delayed, misunderstandings can arise, and opportunities can be missed.

Think about it this way: Imagine trying to build a house without communicating with your team. You'd have architects designing one thing, contractors building another, and suppliers delivering who-knows-what. It would be chaos! But when everyone communicates effectively, sharing plans, asking questions, and providing feedback, the project flows smoothly, resulting in a sturdy, well-built house.

That's why communication is so significant in business operations. It's the foundation upon which everything else is built. Effective communication is key to success, whether we're brainstorming new ideas, negotiating deals, or simply checking in with our teams. As a business owner, it's my responsibility to ensure that communication flows freely and efficiently throughout my organization.

Communication isn't just about talking or sending emails. It's the glue that holds my business together. When my team communicates well, we're like a well-oiled machine. We collaborate, share ideas, and work toward our goals together.

Take collaboration, for example. It's all about working together toward a common goal. And how do we do that? Through communication. When my team members communicate effectively, they can share their thoughts and ideas, bounce them off each other, and come up with creative solutions to problems. It's like a brainstorming session where everyone's voice is heard, and we can tap into the collective wisdom of the group.

Sharing information is another big part of communication. Whether it's updates on projects, customer feedback, or new developments in the industry, sharing information keeps everyone in the loop. And when everyone's on the same page, we can make better decisions, avoid misunderstandings, and confidently move forward.

Perhaps most importantly, communication helps us achieve our organizational goals. Whether it's increasing sales, launching a new product, or expanding into new markets, effective communication is essential every step of the way. It's how we align our efforts, coordinate our actions, and stay focused on the big picture.

Communication isn't just a nice-to-have in business—it's a must-have. It's what keeps us connected, productive, and moving forward toward success. As a business owner, it's my job to foster a culture of open, honest communication where everyone feels valued and heard.

In my business, communication comes in many forms, and each one plays a crucial role in how we operate. First up, we've got verbal communication. This is the good old-fashioned talking—the conversations we have in meetings, over the phone, or even just chatting with colleagues in the hallway. Verbal communication is great because it's quick, direct, and allows for instant feedback. When discussing something important with my team or discussing a new idea, verbal communication is usually my go-to.

Then, there's written communication. This includes emails, memos, reports, and any other written documents we use to convey information. Written communication is handy because it provides a record of what was said and allows people to digest information at their own pace. Plus, it's essential for formalizing agreements or documenting important decisions. Written communication is the way to go when I need to share detailed information or keep a record of our discussions.

Finally, there's non-verbal communication. This one's a bit trickier because it's all about the messages we send without saying a word. It includes things like body language, facial expressions, and even the tone of our voice. Non-verbal communication can convey a lot of information, sometimes even more than words alone. That's why paying attention to how we're coming across is crucial, especially in situations like presentations or client meetings.

In my business, we rely on a mix of verbal, written, and non-verbal communication to keep things running smoothly. Each form has its strengths and weaknesses, but together, they help us stay connected, informed, and on track toward our goals.

In this book, I'll share with you the strategies, tips, and insights I've learned throughout my journey as a business owner. Communication is at the heart of everything we do, from fostering collaboration to sharing information and achieving organizational goals. Join me as we explore the importance of communication in business and learn how to harness its power to drive success in your own entrepreneurial endeavors. Whether you're a seasoned entrepreneur or just starting out, this book will equip you with the skills you need to communicate effectively and take your business to new heights. Let's dive in!

1

UNDERSTANDING THE POWER
OF COMMUNICATION

THE IMPACT OF EFFECTIVE COMMUNICATION

Effective communication is the cornerstone of any successful organization. It's not just about transmitting information—it's about creating an environment where ideas flow freely, collaboration thrives, and goals are achieved efficiently. In my experience as a business owner, I've seen firsthand how effective communication can make or break a company.

When communication is clear and transparent, it fosters trust among team members and with customers alike. Employees feel valued and informed, leading to higher morale and increased productivity. On the other hand, customers appreciate companies that communicate openly and honestly, building loyalty and long-term relationships.

Take, for example, a case study from the retail industry. A company that communicates effectively with its customers providing clear product information, addressing concerns

1

JASON MILLER

promptly, and seeking feedback improves customer satisfaction and gains a competitive edge in the market. By listening to their customers and responding to their needs, this company builds a loyal customer base and sets itself apart from competitors who may not prioritize communication.

In another industry, such as manufacturing, effective communication among team members is essential for ensuring smooth operations and meeting production deadlines. When everyone understands their roles and responsibilities and information is communicated clearly and promptly, it reduces the likelihood of errors and delays, ultimately leading to increased efficiency and profitability.

Overall, the impact of effective communication on organizational success cannot be overstated. By fostering trust, enhancing productivity, and reducing misunderstandings, businesses gain a competitive advantage that sets them apart in today's fast-paced and competitive marketplace. Throughout this book, we'll explore strategies and best practices for improving communication in your organization, helping you unlock its full potential for success.

COMMUNICATION CHALLENGES IN BUSINESS

In the world of business, communication isn't always smooth sailing. We face a myriad of challenges that can throw a wrench in our plans and hinder our progress. One of the biggest hurdles is identifying and overcoming common communication barriers.

Let's say you're leading a diverse team with members from different cultural backgrounds. While diversity brings strength to your organization, it also introduces challenges. Cultural differences, language barriers, and varying communication styles can lead to misunderstandings and misinterpretations.

I've encountered these challenges firsthand in my own business. When team members don't speak the same language fluently or come from different cultural backgrounds, ensuring everyone is on the same page can be challenging. Miscommunications can occur, leading to project delays, conflicts among team members, and decreased productivity.

But it's not just cultural and language barriers that pose a threat to effective communication. Differences in communication styles, such as being direct versus indirect, can also create tension and confusion. For instance, what may seem assertive to one person may come across as rudeness to another.

The consequences of poor communication can be significant. Conflicts may arise, leading to tension and resentment among team members. Errors and misunderstandings can result in costly mistakes, impacting the business's bottom line. And ultimately, decreased productivity can hinder the organization's ability to achieve its goals and compete in the marketplace.

Navigating these communication challenges requires awareness, adaptability, and effective communication strategies. This book will explore practical tips and techniques for overcoming these barriers and fostering a culture of clear and effective communication in your organization. By addressing these challenges head-on, we can unlock the full potential of our teams and drive success in our businesses.

INTERNAL COMMUNICATION SYSTEMS

Imagine running a business without effective communication among your team members—it's like trying to navigate a ship without a compass. Internal communication systems are the backbone of any organization, playing a crucial role in facilitating collaboration, sharing information, and driving productivity.

In my own business, I've come to realize the importance of having robust internal communication systems in place. When everyone is on the same page, and information flows freely, we can work together seamlessly toward our common goals. It's like having a well-oiled machine where every part works in harmony.

But what exactly are internal communication systems? Well, they encompass a range of tools and platforms that enable team members to communicate and collaborate effectively. From traditional methods like email to modern instant messaging apps and project management software, there's no shortage of options available.

Each tool serves its purpose, and choosing the right ones depends on your team's unique needs and preferences. For instance, email may be ideal for formal communications or sharing important documents, while instant messaging apps like Slack or Microsoft Teams are perfect for quick updates and informal chats.

Implementing internal communication systems isn't just about selecting the latest and greatest tools—it's about creating a culture of communication within your organization. That means establishing clear channels for communication, setting expectations around response times, and fostering an environment where team members feel comfortable sharing ideas and feedback.

In my experience, some best practices for implementing internal communication systems include regular check-ins with team members, providing training on how to use new tools effectively, and encouraging open and transparent communication at all levels of the organization.

Investing in robust internal communication systems and adopting best practices can enhance team cohesion, improve efficiency, and ultimately drive success in your business. After all, communication is the key to unlocking the full potential of your team and achieving your business objectives.

EXTERNAL COMMUNICATION SYSTEMS

Communicating effectively with customers, clients, and stakeholders is vital in any business. External communication systems are the tools and processes we use to interact with people outside our organization, and they play a crucial role in building relationships and driving business growth.

In my experience, managing external communication channels can be challenging. With so many ways for people to reach out—whether it's through email, phone calls, or social media—it can be tough to keep track of everything and ensure a consistent message across all channels.

Take email, for example. It's one of the most common ways for customers to contact us, but it's also easy for messages to get lost in the shuffle or for responses to be delayed. Then there's the phone, where customers expect prompt answers and personalized service. And let's not forget about social media, where complaints and inquiries can go viral in an instant.

To navigate these challenges, it's essential to have strategies in place for streamlining our external communication processes. That might mean using tools like customer relationship management (CRM) software to track interactions and centralize customer data. It could also involve establishing clear protocols for responding to inquiries and resolving issues across different channels.

Consistency is key when it comes to external communication. Whether a customer reaches out via email, phone, or social media, they should receive the same level of service and attention to detail. That means training our team members to communicate effectively and ensuring they have the resources they need to do their jobs well.

By implementing these strategies and investing in our external communication systems, we can strengthen our relationships with customers and clients, build trust and loyalty, and ultimately drive success in our business. After all, communication isn't just about conveying information—it's about building connections and creating positive experiences for everyone we interact with.

THE EVOLUTION OF COMMUNICATION TECHNOLOGY

Over the years, communication technology has come a long way, revolutionizing the way businesses interact and operate. Looking back, it's fascinating to see how far we've come and how these advancements have shaped the landscape of business communication.

Let's rewind the clock a bit. Back in the day, businesses relied on traditional methods of communication, like letters, telegraphs, and landline phones. While these methods served their purpose, they were often slow, cumbersome, and limited in reach.

Then came along the internet, and everything changed. With the advent of email, businesses suddenly had a faster, more efficient way to communicate with customers, clients, and colleagues. No longer were we bound by the constraints of snail mail or the time zone differences of international phone calls. Email opened up a whole new world of possibilities for businesses, allowing us to instantly connect with people around the globe.

But the evolution of communication technology didn't stop there. The rise of mobile devices like smartphones and tablets brought communication right to our fingertips, allowing us to stay connected on the go. Suddenly, we weren't tied to our desks anymore—we could respond to emails, make calls, and access important documents from anywhere, at any time.

And then there's social media, arguably one of the most significant developments in recent years. Platforms like Facebook, Twitter, and LinkedIn have transformed the way businesses engage with their audience, providing new avenues for marketing, customer service, and brand building. With social media, businesses can now interact with customers in real time, respond to inquiries and feedback, and showcase their products and services to a global audience.

Looking ahead, the future of business communication looks bright. Emerging technologies like artificial intelligence, virtual reality, and augmented reality have the potential to further revolutionize how we communicate and collaborate. Imagine virtual meetings where participants from around the world can interact in a lifelike environment or AI-powered chatbots that can instantly assist customers with inquiries and support requests.

As business owners, staying abreast of these technological advancements and embracing the opportunities they present is essential. By leveraging the latest communication technologies, we can streamline our operations, improve efficiency, and stay ahead of the competition in today's fast-paced business world. After all, in business, as in life, communication is key.

COMMUNICATION ETHICS AND ETIQUETTE

In business, communication isn't just about exchanging messages—it's about building relationships, fostering trust, and upholding ethical standards. As a business owner, I understand the importance of maintaining integrity in all aspects of communication.

Ethics play a crucial role in business communication. It's not just about what we say—it's about how we say it and the values we uphold. Honesty, transparency, and respect for privacy are non-negotiables in my book. Whether it's communicating with customers, clients, or colleagues, I believe in being upfront and truthful, even when it's difficult. After all, trust is the foundation of any successful business relationship, and it's built on a bedrock of honesty.

But ethics go beyond just being truthful. It's also about practicing good communication etiquette. This means being an active listener, speaking clearly and concisely, and always conducting oneself with professionalism. As a business owner, I strive to lead by example, demonstrating respect and courtesy in every interaction.

Of course, navigating ethical dilemmas isn't always easy. There are times when we may face tough decisions or conflicting priorities. In those moments, it's essential to pause, reflect, and consider the consequences of our actions. We can navigate these challenges with integrity and grace by staying true to our values and principles.

Communication ethics and etiquette aren't just nice-to-haves—they're essential to successful business practices. By prioritizing honesty, transparency, and respect in our communication, we can build stronger relationships, foster trust, and, ultimately, drive business success.

Conclusion

As I wrap up this chapter, I want to take a moment to summarize the key ideas we've covered. We've explored communication's fundamental role in business operations, from fostering collaboration among team members to interacting with customers and stakeholders. We've discussed the various forms of internal and external communication and the challenges that can arise in navigating these channels effectively.

Throughout our discussion, one thing has become abundantly clear: effective communication is the cornerstone of success in business. It's not just about exchanging words—it's about building relationships, fostering trust, and driving organizational goals forward.

As a business owner, I've seen firsthand the impact that clear and transparent communication can have on productivity, morale, and, ultimately, the bottom line. By understanding the power of communication and investing in the right systems and strategies, we can set ourselves up for success in today's fast-paced business environment.

The next chapter will dive deeper into internal communication systems and strategies, exploring how we can enhance team cohesion, streamline processes, and drive greater efficiency. I'm excited to continue this journey with you as we explore the tools and techniques that can help us communicate more effectively and achieve our business objectives.

2
INTERNAL COMMUNICATION STRATEGIES

INTRODUCTION TO INTERNAL COMMUNICATION

Internal communication is the lifeblood of any successful business. It's the glue that holds teams together, ensuring everyone is on the same page and working toward common goals. But what exactly is internal communication, and why is it so important?

In simple terms, internal communication refers to the exchange of information and ideas within an organization. It encompasses everything from team meetings and memos to email exchanges and instant messaging. Essentially, it's how we communicate with our colleagues, managers, and employees on a day-to-day basis.

However, internal communication is more than just passing messages back and forth. It plays a vital role in fostering collaboration among team members, allowing them to work together effectively toward shared objectives. When communication channels are open and transparent, it becomes easier for employees to share ideas, seek feedback, and coordinate their efforts toward achieving organizational goals.

Think of internal communication as the engine that drives productivity and efficiency within a company. Without it, teams would struggle to stay organized, projects would fall behind schedule, and morale would suffer. In short, effective internal communication is essential for keeping the wheels of business turning smoothly.

Types of Internal Communication

In my business, internal communication happens in various ways. There's the face-to-face chatter during team meetings or casual catchups in the break room. Then there's the written stuff, like emails, memos, and notices pinned on the bulletin board. And, of course, we rely heavily on digital communication tools like instant messaging apps and project management software in today's digital age.

Each type of communication has its perks and drawbacks. When we're talking face-to-face, it's great for building rapport and getting instant feedback. But it can also be time-consuming, especially if everyone has busy schedules.

On the other hand, written communication is handy for documenting important information and keeping records. Plus, it's easier to distribute documents and announcements to a large group of people. However, written messages can sometimes lack the personal touch of face-to-face interactions, and there's always the risk of misinterpretation.

Then there's digital communication, which has become a game-changer for businesses in recent years. Platforms like

Slack and Microsoft Teams allow us to communicate in real time, no matter where we are. It's incredibly convenient, especially for remote teams or those with members spread across different locations. But there's also the danger of information overload, with messages flooding in from multiple channels and distractions pulling us away from important tasks.

Ultimately, each communication method has its place in the business world. The key is knowing when to use each one effectively and finding the right balance to keep everyone connected and informed.

INTERNAL COMMUNICATION PLATFORMS

In my business, we've tried several internal communication platforms over the years. Each one has its pros and cons, and finding the right fit for our team has been a bit of a journey.

First up, there's email. It's the old faithful of communication tools, and it's great for sending out formal announcements or sharing detailed information that needs to be documented. Almost everyone knows how to use it, so there's not much of a learning curve. But it can get overwhelming fast, with inboxes filling up and important messages getting buried under piles of junk.

Then there's instant messaging. We use platforms like Slack and Microsoft Teams for real-time communication, whether quick questions, brainstorming sessions, or just shooting the breeze with coworkers. It's great for keeping conversations organized and searchable, but it can also be a bit too informal sometimes, with memes and emojis flying left and right.

Finally, there's project management software. Tools like Asana and Trello help us prioritize our tasks and collaborate on projects more efficiently. They're perfect for keeping everyone on the same page and tracking progress, but they can also be a bit overwhelming with all their bells and whistles.

When it comes down to it, the best internal communication platform for us is one that strikes the right balance between features, usability, and suitability for our specific needs. It's all about finding the tool that helps us communicate effectively without getting in the way of getting things done.

Best Practices for Effective Internal Communication

In my experience running a business, I've found that effective internal communication is key to keeping things running smoothly. Over the years, I've picked up a few best practices that have helped us foster better communication among our team members.

First and foremost, transparency is crucial. We make it a point to share information openly and honestly with everyone on the team. Whether it's updates on company goals, policy changes, or even just sharing wins and challenges, keeping everyone in the loop helps build trust and keeps everyone on the same page.

Clarity is another big one. When it comes to communication, clarity is king. We keep our messages simple and straightforward, avoiding jargon or overly technical language whenever possible. This helps ensure that everyone

14

understands what's being communicated and reduces the chances of misunderstandings.

Accessibility is also important. We use a variety of communication channels to reach different team members, including email, instant messaging, and project management software. By providing multiple channels for communication, we make it easier for everyone to stay connected and engaged, no matter where they are or what they're working on.

Finally, we encourage active listening and feedback. Communication is a two-way street, and it's important for everyone on the team to feel heard and valued. We make it a point to listen to our team members' input and ideas, and we're always open to feedback on how we can improve our communication processes.

Following these best practices has created a culture of open communication and collaboration within our organization. As a result, we've seen improved productivity, better teamwork, and, ultimately, greater success as a business.

Overcoming Internal Communication Challenges

In running my business, I've encountered various challenges regarding internal communication. From dealing with silos to overcoming miscommunication and information overload, there have been times when keeping everyone on the same page has felt like a real struggle.

One of the biggest challenges we've faced is silos – those invisible barriers that can develop between different teams or departments within an organization. When information gets trapped in these silos, it can lead to misunderstandings, dupli-cation of effort, and missed opportunities for collaboration.

To tackle this challenge, we've worked hard to foster a culture of openness and collaboration across the entire orga-nization. We encourage team members to share information freely and to reach out to colleagues in other departments whenever they need input or assistance. By breaking down these silos and encouraging cross-functional communication, we've been able to improve collaboration and streamline our operations.

Another common challenge is miscommunication. Whether it's a simple misunderstanding or a breakdown in communication processes, miscommunication can lead to all sorts of problems – from missed deadlines to costly errors.

To address this challenge, we've strongly emphasized clarity and transparency in our communication practices. We ensure that everyone understands their roles and responsibilities and provide clear guidelines for how information should be shared and communicated within the organization. We also encourage open dialogue and feedback so team members feel comfortable speaking up if they have questions or concerns.

Finally, there's the issue of information overload. In today's fast-paced business environment, it's easy to feel overwhelmed by the sheer volume of emails, messages, and notifications that come our way every day.

To help our team members manage this overload, we've implemented strategies like setting clear priorities, establishing regular communication routines, and using tools like project management software to keep track of tasks and deadlines. We also encourage mindfulness and self-care, reminding everyone to take breaks and unplug when needed to avoid burnout.

By addressing these internal communication challenges head-on and implementing strategies to overcome them, we've created a more cohesive and productive work environment for our team. And as a result, we've seen improvements in everything from employee satisfaction to overall business performance.

Implementing Internal Communication Strategies

Implementing effective internal communication strategies has been a cornerstone of success in my business. Over the years, I've learned that fostering open communication and collaboration within teams is crucial, regardless of the organization's size.

One key aspect of implementing these strategies is to lead by example. As a business owner, I make it a point to communicate openly and transparently with my team members. I encourage them to ask questions, share ideas, and voice their concerns without fear of judgment. I set the tone for the entire organization by demonstrating a commitment to open communication.

Another important step is to establish clear communication channels and processes. This means defining how information flows within the organization, setting expectations for how and when team members should communicate, and providing the necessary tools and resources to support effective communication. Whether through regular team meetings, project management software, or instant messaging platforms, having well-defined communication channels helps ensure everyone is on the same page.

Creating a culture of open communication and collaboration also requires fostering trust and respect among team members. This means creating an environment where everyone feels valued and heard, regardless of their position or title. Encouraging active listening, acknowledging contributions, and celebrating achievements are all ways to promote a positive and supportive workplace culture.

Finally, it's important to continuously evaluate and adjust communication strategies as needed. This means soliciting feedback from team members, monitoring the effectiveness of communication channels, and making improvements based on what works best for the organization. By staying flexible and responsive to the team's evolving needs, we can ensure that our internal communication strategies remain effective and impactful.

CASE STUDIES AND EXAMPLES

In my journey as a business owner, I've come across numerous case studies and real-life examples that highlight the importance of effective internal communication. These stories offer valuable insights into how different organizations have successfully implemented strategies to enhance team communication.

One such example comes from a tech startup I admire. They recognized early on that fostering a culture of open communication was essential for innovation and collaboration. To achieve this, they implemented regular team meetings where employees were encouraged to share their ideas and provide feedback on ongoing projects. This approach led to the generation of creative solutions and helped build a sense of camaraderie among team members.

Another inspiring case study comes from a large manufacturing company. Facing challenges with siloed communication and information overload, they decided to streamline their internal communication processes. They invested in project management software that enabled teams to collaborate more effectively and stay organized. By centralizing communication and providing clear channels for sharing information, they were able to improve productivity and reduce errors in their operations.

These examples demonstrate that successful internal communication strategies are not one-size-fits-all. Instead, they are tailored to each organization's unique needs and challenges. By learning from these case studies and applying their lessons, businesses can develop strategies for fostering effective communication within their teams. Whether it's through regular meetings, digital tools, or a combination of both, the key is to prioritize transparency, collaboration, and open dialogue.

Conclusion

As I reflect on the insights gained from exploring internal communication in this chapter, I'm reminded of its fundamental role in the success of any organization. Effective internal communication is the backbone of a thriving business, from fostering collaboration and sharing information to achieving organizational goals.

Throughout our discussion, we've uncovered various types of internal communication methods, platforms, and best practices. We've examined the challenges businesses face in this area and explored strategies for overcoming them. Additionally, we've delved into real-life case studies that showcase successful internal communication strategies in action.

At its core, internal communication is about more than just exchanging messages—it's about creating a culture of openness, transparency, and collaboration within teams. By implementing effective communication strategies, businesses can streamline operations, boost productivity, and foster a sense of unity among employees.

As we look ahead to the next chapter, we'll shift our focus to external communication strategies. Just as internal communication is vital for collaboration within the organization, external communication is essential for building relationships with customers, clients, and stakeholders. We'll explore the tools, tactics, and best practices for effectively communicating with external audiences and driving business growth.

3

EXTERNAL COMMUNICATION STRATEGIES

INTRODUCTION TO EXTERNAL COMMUNICATION

External communication is the lifeline of any business. It's how we connect with the world outside our organization—customers, clients, stakeholders, you name it. Think of it as the bridge that links us to the people who matter most to our success.

When we talk about external communication, we talk about everything we do to reach beyond our company walls. It's the emails we send to customers, the phone calls we make to clients, the posts we share on social media, and even the face-to-face meetings we have with stakeholders.

This communication isn't just about exchanging information; it's about building relationships. Every interaction we have with someone outside our organization is an opportunity to connect, to understand their needs, and to show them why they should choose us over the competition.

External communication plays a crucial role in shaping how others perceive us, whether we're introducing a new product, addressing a customer complaint, or negotiating a deal with a client. It's our chance to make a positive impression, to build trust, and to demonstrate our value.

In short, external communication isn't just about talking; it's about building relationships that drive our business forward. It's about showing the world who we are, what we stand for, and why we're the best choice for their needs.

TYPES OF EXTERNAL COMMUNICATION

When it comes to communicating with folks outside our business, we've got a bunch of different tools in our toolbox. Each one has its own strengths and weaknesses, like different tools you might use for different jobs around the house.

Let's start with good old-fashioned email. It's like sending a letter, but way faster. Email is great because it's quick and easy, and you can send it to lots of people all at once. Plus, you've got a record of what you said in case you need to refer to it later. The downside? Sometimes, emails can get lost in the shuffle, and it's not always the best way to have a real-time conversation.

Then there's the trusty phone call. You can't beat the personal touch of hearing someone's voice on the other end of the line. Phone calls are great for having more in-depth conversations or for situations where you need to talk through something quickly. But they can also be a bit intrusive, especially if you catch someone at a bad time.

Social media is another big one these days. Platforms like Facebook, Twitter, and LinkedIn are great for reaching a wide audience and engaging with customers in real time. They're a great way to show off your personality and build your brand. But, of course, social media can also be a bit of a double-edged sword. It's easy for things to get misinterpreted or blown out of proportion, and you've got to be careful about what you post.

Finally, there are good old-fashioned face-to-face meetings. There's nothing quite like sitting down with someone and having a conversation in person. It's great for building rapport and really getting to know someone. But, of course, it can also be time-consuming and expensive, especially if you've got to travel to meet with someone.

So, each communication method has its pros and cons, and the key is figuring out which is best for the situation. Sometimes, it might even be a combination of a few different methods that get the job done best.

EXTERNAL COMMUNICATION CHANNELS

When it comes to talking to folks outside of our business, we've got plenty of tools at our disposal. You know, like different channels on a TV, each with its own shows and audience.

First up, there's email marketing. It's like sending out a bunch of flyers to people's mailboxes, except it's all done digitally. With email marketing, we can reach a lot of people all at once and tailor our messages to specific groups. Plus, we can track things like open rates and click-through rates to see how effective our emails are. But, you know, sometimes people's inboxes get pretty crowded, so it can be tough to stand out.

Then there's social media. Platforms like Facebook, Twitter, and Instagram are like giant virtual bulletin boards where people hang out and share stuff. We can use social media to connect with our audience, share updates and promotions, and even run ads to reach new customers. The cool thing about social media is that it's a two-way street - we can interact with our customers and get real-time feedback. However, it can also be a bit of a Wild West out there, with lots of noise and competition for attention.

Another tool in our toolbox is customer relationship management (CRM) systems. These are like digital Rolodexes on steroids, helping us keep track of all our interactions with customers and prospects. With a CRM, we can store contact information, track sales leads, and even automate certain tasks like sending follow-up emails. It's a great way to stay organized and keep our finger on the pulse of our business relationships. But, you know, setting up and maintaining a CRM system can be a bit of a project, and it's only as good as the data we put into it.

Each external communication channel has its strengths and weaknesses, and the key is figuring out which ones work best for our business and our audience. It might be a combination of a few different channels that gets the job done best.

BEST PRACTICES FOR EFFECTIVE EXTERNAL COMMUNICATION

When talking to our customers, clients, and other folks outside of our business, there are some tried-and-true ways to ensure we're hitting the mark.

First off, consistency is key. We want to ensure our messaging is consistent across all our external communication channels, whether our website, social media pages, or email newsletters. That way, people know what to expect from us and can trust that we're reliable.

Clarity is another big one. We want to keep our messages clear and easy to understand without jargon or confusing language. Whether writing an email or posting on social media, we want to ensure our audience knows exactly what we're trying to say.

Professionalism is also important. Even if we're posting on social media or sending out a casual email, we want to maintain a level of professionalism that reflects well on our business. That means using proper grammar and spelling, promptly responding to inquiries, and treating our customers and clients with respect.

By following these best practices, we can make sure our external communication is effective and helps us build strong relationships with our customers, clients, and stakeholders.

Overcoming External Communication Challenges

When it comes to chatting with folks outside of our business, there can be some hurdles to clear. Language barriers, cultural differences, and just too much information flying around can all make it tricky to get our message across.

Take language barriers, for instance. If we're dealing with customers or clients who speak a different language, we might need to find ways to bridge that gap. That could mean using translation tools or hiring bilingual staff to help out.

Then, there are cultural differences. What's considered polite or appropriate in one culture might not fly in another. So, we need to be mindful of cultural nuances and adapt our communication style accordingly.

And let's not forget about information overload. With emails, texts, phone calls, and social media notifications constantly bombarding us, it's easy for important messages to get lost in the shuffle. That's why it's crucial to streamline our communication channels and prioritize the most important messages.

But fear not! There are ways to overcome these challenges and make sure our external communication is as effective as possible. It might take a bit of creativity and flexibility, but with the right strategies in place, we can navigate these obstacles and keep the conversation flowing smoothly.

IMPLEMENTING EXTERNAL COMMUNICATION STRATEGIES

When it comes to reaching out to our customers and clients, having a solid plan in place is key. We want to make sure we're engaging with them in a way that keeps them happy and coming back for more.

So, how do we do that? First, we need to figure out what channels work best for us. That might mean using email, social media, or even good old-fashioned phone calls. Once we've sorted our channels, we can start crafting our messages.

It's important to keep things consistent across all our communication channels. That means using the same tone and style no matter where we're reaching out. We want our customers to know exactly what to expect from us, whether they're reading an email or checking out our latest post on social media.

And don't forget about timing. We want to make sure we're reaching out to our customers at the right time when they're most likely to be receptive to our message. That might mean sending out emails in the morning when they're checking their inbox or posting on social media during peak hours when they're most active.

By integrating all these strategies into a cohesive external communication plan, we can make sure we're hitting all the right notes with our customers and clients. And that's what it's all about – keeping them engaged, satisfied, and returning for more.

Case Studies and Examples

Let me share some stories from the business world to illustrate how effective external communication can make a real difference. Take, for example, a small online clothing store that I came across recently. They struggled to stand out in a crowded market, so they revamped their social media strategy.

Instead of just posting pictures of their products, they started sharing behind-the-scenes glimpses of their design process and engaging with customers in the comments. They even ran some fun contests and giveaways to get people excited about their brand.

Before long, their followers started to grow, and so did their sales. By being more open and interactive on social media, they were able to build stronger relationships with their customers and create a loyal fan base.

Another example comes from a local restaurant that I frequent. They were having trouble getting the word out about their new menu items, so they decided to send out a weekly newsletter to their email subscribers.

Each newsletter would highlight a different dish and share the story behind it, along with some mouthwatering pictures. They also included special offers and discounts to entice people to come in and try the food for themselves.

The response was overwhelming. Not only did they see an increase in foot traffic, but they also got tons of positive feedback from customers who appreciated the personal touch.

These are just a couple of examples of how effective external communication can drive success in business. By being open, engaging, and authentic, you can build strong connections with your customers and keep them returning for more.

CONCLUSION

In wrapping up this chapter, let's recap what we've covered about external communication. We've explored how businesses communicate with customers, whether through emails, phone calls, social media, or face-to-face interactions. Each method has pros and cons, but they all play a vital role in building relationships and driving business growth.

We've also discussed the challenges businesses face when communicating externally, such as language barriers and information overload. But with the right strategies in place, these challenges can be overcome, and communication can become a powerful tool for success.

Effective external communication isn't just about getting your message out there; it's about connecting with your audience on a deeper level. By being transparent, engaging, and responsive, you can build customer trust and loyalty, ultimately leading to increased satisfaction and retention.

As we move forward, we'll shift our focus to communication ethics and professionalism. We'll explore the importance of honesty, integrity, and respect in business communication and how adhering to these principles can strengthen your reputation and build credibility with your stakeholders. So, let's dive into the next chapter and continue our journey toward becoming effective communicators in the business world.

4

COMMUNICATION ETHICS
AND PROFESSIONALISM

In the world of business, communication isn't just about exchanging words or ideas; it's also about doing so in a way that upholds certain ethical standards and professionalism. Let me explain what that means.

Communication ethics, simply put, is about doing the right thing when it comes to how we communicate with others in a business setting. It's about being honest, transparent, and respectful in all our interactions, whether it's with customers, colleagues, or stakeholders. This isn't just a nicety—it's crucial for maintaining trust and credibility in the long run.

Now, let's talk about professionalism. When we say professionalism in communication, we're talking about conducting ourselves in a manner that reflects positively on ourselves and our businesses. It's about being clear, courteous, and considerate in our communication, whether we're speaking face-to-face, sending an email, or making a phone call. Professionalism sets the tone for how others perceive us and can make a big difference in how successful we are in our business endeavors.

In this chapter, we'll explore these concepts of communication ethics and professionalism in more detail, diving into why they matter and how we can uphold them in our day-to-day interactions. Understanding and embodying these principles can improve our relationships with others and contribute to our businesses' overall success.

UNDERSTANDING COMMUNICATION ETHICS

Ethics isn't just a buzzword in business—it's a guiding principle that shapes how we communicate with others. Let's talk about what that means.

When we talk about communication ethics, we're talking about doing the right thing in our interactions with others. That means being honest and truthful in what we say, even when it's not easy. It means being transparent and upfront about our intentions and actions so there's no room for misunderstanding. It means respecting the privacy and confidentiality of others and keeping sensitive information secure and confidential.

Why does this matter? Well, think about it this way: when we communicate ethically, we build trust and credibility with those around us. People know they can rely on us to be honest and transparent, and that goes a long way in establishing strong relationships, whether it's with customers, employees, or business partners. On the flip side, if we're not ethical in our communication, we risk damaging those relationships and losing the trust of others.

So, in this chapter, we will explore these ethical considerations in more detail. We'll talk about why honesty, transparency, and respect for privacy are so important in business communication, and we'll discuss some practical strategies for upholding these principles in our day-to-day interactions. By understanding and embodying communication ethics, we can build stronger relationships and create a more ethical and trustworthy business environment.

PRINCIPLES OF PROFESSIONALISM IN COMMUNICATION

In business, professionalism isn't just about wearing a suit and tie—it's about how we communicate with others. Let's talk about what that looks like.

When we're talking about professionalism in communication, we're talking about how we present ourselves and our ideas to others. That means speaking and writing clearly and concisely so there's no confusion about what we're trying to say. It means being courteous and respectful in our interactions and treating others with kindness and consideration. And it means using tact and diplomacy, especially when dealing with sensitive or difficult topics.

Why does this matter? Well, think about it this way: when we communicate professionally, we respect ourselves and the people we're talking to. We demonstrate that we take our work seriously and that we value the opinions and feelings of others. And that goes a long way in building trust and credibility in our relationships, both inside and outside the workplace.

So, in this chapter, we're going to explore these principles of professionalism in more detail. We'll talk about why clarity, courtesy, and tact are so important in communication, and we'll discuss some practical strategies for embodying these principles in our day-to-day interactions. By embracing professionalism in our communication, we can enhance our reputation and contribute to a more positive and respectful work environment.

ETHICAL DILEMMAS IN BUSINESS COMMUNICATION

Ethical dilemmas in business communication can be like navigating a maze. Sometimes, it's not just about what's right or wrong—it's about finding the best path forward.

In my experience, I've encountered various ethical dilemmas in communication, and they're not always easy to spot. It could be as simple as deciding whether to be completely transparent with a client about a mistake we made, or it could be more complex, like balancing the need for confidentiality with the obligation to report unethical behavior.

One common dilemma is the temptation to embellish or exaggerate the truth to make a sale or win a contract. It can be tempting to stretch the truth a little to make ourselves look better or to secure a deal, but it's essential to remember that honesty and integrity are the cornerstones of ethical communication.

Another challenge arises when we're faced with conflicting interests—like when we have to choose between what's best for our company and what's best for our customers or stakeholders. In these situations, it's crucial to weigh the potential consequences of our actions and consider the long-term impact on our relationships and reputation.

To navigate these ethical dilemmas, I rely on a few guiding principles. First and foremost, I always try to put myself in the other person's shoes and consider how my actions might affect them. I also seek advice from trusted colleagues or mentors and consult company policies and ethical guidelines to ensure I'm making the right decision.

Ultimately, ethical communication is about doing the right thing, even when it's difficult or inconvenient. By staying true to our values and principles, we can build trust and credibility in our relationships and uphold the reputation of our business.

Maintaining Ethical Standards

Maintaining ethical standards in communication is like tending to a garden—you have to nurture it to ensure it grows strong and healthy.

In my business, fostering a culture of ethical communication is paramount. It's not just about following rules; it's about instilling values that guide our interactions with others.

One strategy I've found effective is leading by example. As the leader of my organization, I understand the importance of modeling ethical behavior in all my communications, whether with clients, employees, or stakeholders. By demonstrating honesty, integrity, and respect in my actions, I set the tone for others to follow.

Another key aspect is creating clear communication policies that outline our ethical standards and expectations. These policies serve as a roadmap for employees, helping them understand what's acceptable and what's not in their interactions with others. We regularly review and update these policies to ensure they reflect our values and align with industry best practices.

But it's not enough to just have policies in place—we also need to enforce them consistently. This means holding ourselves and others accountable for adhering to our ethical standards. When issues arise, we address them promptly and transparently, taking appropriate action to rectify any breaches of trust or misconduct.

Ultimately, maintaining ethical standards in communication requires a collective effort. It's about fostering a culture where integrity is valued and rewarded, and everyone feels empowered to speak up if they see something that doesn't align with our values. By prioritizing ethical behavior in our communications, we not only strengthen our relationships with clients and stakeholders but also uphold the reputation and integrity of our organization.

PROFESSIONAL DEVELOPMENT IN COMMUNICATION

In the world of business, communication skills are like muscles—you have to keep exercising them to stay strong and effective.

I've learned firsthand that professional development in communication is crucial for staying ahead in today's competitive landscape. Whether it's honing my presentation skills, mastering the art of negotiation, or improving my written communication, there's always room for growth.

That's why I make it a priority to invest in continuous learning and improvement. I seek resources and training programs to help me sharpen my communication skills and stay up-to-date with the latest trends and best practices. Whether it's attending workshops, enrolling in online courses, or reading books on communication theory, I'm always looking for opportunities to expand my knowledge and expertise.

But professional development isn't just about acquiring new skills—it's also about self-reflection and self-assessment. I take the time to evaluate my strengths and weaknesses in communication, identifying areas where I can improve and setting specific goals for myself. Whether it's becoming a more effective listener, improving my public speaking abilities, or mastering the art of written communication, I'm constantly striving to grow and evolve as a communicator.

By investing in my professional development, I not only enhance my own effectiveness but also contribute to the success of my business. After all, communication is the lifeblood of any organization, and the better we are at it, the more we can achieve together.

Conclusion

As I wrap up this chapter, I'm reminded of the critical role that communication ethics and professionalism play in the success of any business.

Throughout our discussion, we've explored the importance of honesty, transparency, and respect for privacy in communication. We've also touched on the principles of professionalism, emphasizing the value of clarity, courtesy, and tact in our interactions with others.

These concepts may seem simple, but they form the foundation of strong, ethical communication practices. By adhering to ethical standards and maintaining professionalism in our communication, we build trust and credibility with our stakeholders and foster a positive work culture where integrity and respect are valued.

As we move forward, I'm excited to delve deeper into the topic of leveraging communication for leadership and influence. Stay tuned for insights and strategies on how effective communication can empower us to lead with confidence and make a lasting impact on our teams and organizations.

5

LEVERAGING COMMUNICATION FOR LEADERSHIP AND INFLUENCE

In this chapter, I'll be talking about a topic that's near and dear to my heart: leadership communication. Let's kick things off by understanding what exactly we mean by "leadership communication."

When we talk about leadership communication, we're referring to how leaders use their communication skills to guide and inspire others. It's about more than just giving orders or instructions; it's about effectively conveying a vision, motivating team members, and fostering collaboration.

You might be wondering why effective communication is crucial in leadership roles. Well, think about it this way: as a leader, I'm responsible for guiding my team toward our goals, making important decisions, and dealing with any challenges that come our way. And how do I do all of that? Through communication.

Effective communication is the cornerstone of successful leadership, whether it's communicating expectations, providing feedback, or resolving conflicts. It helps me build trust and credibility with my team, keep everyone aligned and motivated, and ultimately, achieve our objectives.

So, throughout this chapter, we'll explore the various aspects of leadership communication, from essential skills to successful strategies. Because when it comes down to it, effective leadership starts with effective communication.

LEADERSHIP COMMUNICATION SKILLS

Regarding leadership, communication skills are at the top of my list. Let's talk about some key ones that I rely on daily.

First up is active listening. It's not just about hearing what others are saying; it's about fully engaging with them, understanding their perspectives, and showing that I value their input. Whether it's a team member sharing an idea or a client expressing a concern, active listening helps me build stronger relationships and make better-informed decisions.

Next, empathy is essential. Putting myself in someone else's shoes helps me connect with my team on a deeper level. It shows them that I understand their feelings and challenges, which fosters trust and loyalty. Plus, it's a crucial skill for resolving conflicts and building a supportive work environment.

Assertiveness is another key skill. It's about expressing my thoughts and opinions clearly and confidently while also respecting others' perspectives. Assertive communication helps me set expectations, delegate tasks, and address issues head-on, which is crucial for effective leadership.

Of course, clarity and conciseness are vital too. As a leader, I need to communicate complex ideas and instructions in a way that everyone can understand. Keeping my messages clear and to the point helps avoid misunderstandings and keeps everyone on the same page.

Adaptability rounds out the list. In today's fast-paced business world, things can change in an instant. Being able to adapt my communication style to different situations and audiences ensures that I can effectively lead my team through any challenges that come our way.

Overall, these communication skills are the foundation of effective leadership. I can inspire, motivate, and guide my team toward success by honing these abilities.

COMMUNICATION STRATEGIES FOR LEADERSHIP SUCCESS

In my journey as a leader, I've come to rely on certain communication strategies that have proven crucial for success. Let me share some of them with you.

First and foremost, clear goal-setting and direction are essential. As a leader, it's my responsibility to provide a clear vision of where we're headed and what we aim to achieve. This clarity helps align everyone's efforts toward a common objective, ensuring we're all moving in the same direction.

Inspiring and motivating team members is another key strategy. I've learned that people are more likely to give their best when they feel inspired and valued. I can create a positive and motivating work environment that drives success by recognizing their contributions, highlighting their strengths, and encouraging them to reach their full potential.

Providing constructive feedback is also crucial. Whether it's praise for a job well done or guidance for improvement, feedback helps my team members grow and develop professionally. I strive to offer feedback in a constructive and supportive manner, focusing on specific behaviors or outcomes and offering actionable suggestions for improvement.

Delegating tasks effectively is another skill I've honed over time. As a leader, I can't do everything myself, nor should I. Delegating tasks allows me to leverage the strengths and talents of my team members, empowering them to take ownership of their work and contribute to our collective success.

Of course, conflicts and difficult conversations are inevitable in any workplace. Learning how to handle them with grace and professionalism is key. I've found that addressing conflicts head-on, actively listening to all parties involved, and seeking mutually beneficial solutions can help resolve issues and strengthen relationships within the team.

These communication strategies have been instrumental in my journey as a leader. By setting clear goals, inspiring and motivating my team, providing constructive feedback, delegating tasks effectively, and handling conflicts with professionalism, I've been able to lead my team toward success while fostering a positive and collaborative work environment.

LEADING THROUGH CHANGE AND UNCERTAINTY

Leading through change and uncertainty is one of the most challenging aspects of leadership, but it's also where effective communication truly shines.

In my experience, communication plays a pivotal role in navigating turbulent times. When faced with change, whether it's a shift in strategy, restructuring, or market fluctuations, I've learned that transparency and honesty are non-negotiable. Keeping my team informed about what's happening, why it's happening, and how it will impact them builds trust and reduces anxiety.

Active engagement and involvement are also crucial during times of change. Instead of simply dictating decisions from the top down, I make it a point to involve my team in the process. By soliciting their input, listening to their concerns, and involving them in decision-making, I empower them to take ownership of the change and become active participants in shaping the future of our organization.

Providing support and reassurance is another essential aspect of leading through uncertainty. Change can be unsettling, and it's natural for team members to feel anxious or uncertain about the future. As a leader, I strive to be a source of support, offering guidance, encouragement, and reassurance to help my team navigate through uncertainty with confidence and resilience.

Throughout my career, I've encountered numerous examples of successful leadership during periods of change. From companies that successfully pivoted their business models to adapt to changing market conditions to leaders who effectively communicated with their teams during times of crisis, these case studies serve as valuable lessons in the power of effective communication in navigating change and uncertainty.

Ultimately, leading through change and uncertainty requires a combination of clear communication, active engagement, and unwavering support. By embracing these strategies and learning from real-life examples of successful leadership, I've been able to guide my team through even the most challenging of times, emerging stronger and more resilient on the other side.

Building Influence Through Communication

In my journey as a business owner, I've understood the pivotal role of effective communication in building influence and authority. It's not just about what I say but how I say it and its impact on those around me.

One of the key strategies I've found to be effective in building influence is establishing credibility and trust. People are more likely to listen to and follow someone they trust and perceive as credible. To achieve this, I focus on consistency in my messaging, ensuring that my words align with my actions and values. By consistently delivering on promises and demonstrating integrity in all my interactions, I earn my team's and stakeholders' trust.

Demonstrating expertise and knowledge is another important aspect of building influence. When I communicate, whether it's in meetings, presentations, or written communications, I make sure to draw on my expertise and knowledge to provide valuable insights and solutions. By showcasing my expertise in my field, I establish myself as a credible authority and someone worth listening to.

Building rapport and relationships is also key to building influence. I invest time and effort in getting to know my team members, clients, and stakeholders on a personal level, building genuine connections based on mutual respect and understanding. By fostering strong relationships, I not only gain the trust and support of those around me but also create a network of allies who can help me achieve my goals.

Furthermore, I've found the power of storytelling and persuasion to be invaluable in building influence. By weaving compelling narratives and using persuasive techniques, I can effectively communicate my ideas, inspire action, and influence others to buy into my vision.

Building influence through communication is about more than just the words we speak. It's about building trust, demonstrating expertise, fostering relationships, and using persuasive storytelling to inspire action and drive change. By mastering these strategies, I've been able to elevate my influence and authority as a business owner, leading to greater success and impact in my endeavors.

COMMUNICATION CHALLENGES IN LEADERSHIP

As a business owner, I've encountered my fair share of communication challenges in leadership roles. These challenges can arise from various factors, and addressing them effectively is essential for maintaining effectiveness as a leader.

One common communication challenge I've faced is misalignment among team members. When everyone isn't on the same page or working toward the same goals, it can lead to confusion, inefficiency, and, ultimately, missed opportunities. To overcome this challenge, I prioritize clear and consistent communication, ensuring everyone understands the objectives, expectations, and roles within the team. I can keep everyone aligned and moving in the right direction by fostering open dialogue and providing regular updates.

Resistance to change is another significant communication challenge in leadership. When introducing new initiatives or implementing changes within the organization, resistance from team members can hinder progress and undermine the initiative's success. To address this challenge, I approach change management with empathy and understanding, acknowledging the concerns and perspectives of team members. I can mitigate resistance and facilitate smoother transitions by involving them in the decision-making process, providing ample communication about the rationale behind the changes, and offering support and resources for adaptation.

Communication breakdowns are also a common challenge that can impede leadership effectiveness. Whether it's due to misunderstandings, conflicting priorities, or simply lapses in communication, breakdowns can lead to errors, delays, and frustration among team members. I prioritize clarity, transparency, and active listening to prevent and address communication breakdowns. I encourage open communication channels where team members feel comfortable voicing their concerns, asking questions, and providing feedback. Additionally, I remain vigilant for signs of communication breakdowns and address them promptly through clear communication and problem-solving.

In navigating these communication challenges, I've learned that proactive communication, empathy, and a willingness to address issues head-on are key. By fostering a culture of open communication, understanding, and collaboration, I can overcome challenges, maintain effectiveness as a leader, and lead my team toward success.

LEADING REMOTE AND VIRTUAL TEAMS

Leading remote and virtual teams has become increasingly common in today's business landscape, presenting both challenges and opportunities for effective communication. As a business owner who has transitioned to leading remote teams, I've had to adapt my communication strategies to ensure continued success and productivity.

One of the most significant challenges of leading remote teams is the lack of face-to-face interaction. Without the ability to communicate in person, building rapport, establishing trust, and conveying nuance in conversations can be more challenging. To overcome this challenge, I leverage technology to facilitate regular video conferences and virtual meetings. Seeing each other's faces and body language allows my team and I to maintain a sense of connection and collaboration, even when miles apart.

Another challenge of remote leadership is ensuring clear and effective communication across different time zones and schedules. With team members scattered across various locations, coordinating meetings and ensuring everyone is on the same page can be a logistical challenge. I utilize asynchronous communication tools such as email, messaging apps, and project management software to address this. These tools allow team members to communicate and collaborate on their own schedules, ensuring that important information is accessible to everyone, regardless of time zone differences.

Despite these challenges, leading remote teams also presents unique opportunities for fostering collaboration, engagement, and productivity. Remote work allows for greater flexibility and autonomy, which can lead to increased job satisfaction and creativity among team members. To capitalize on these opportunities, I encourage open communication channels, regular check-ins, and opportunities for virtual team-building activities. By fostering a culture of trust, autonomy, and accountability, I empower my remote team members to thrive in their roles and contribute to the business's success.

I've learned that effective communication is paramount in navigating the complexities of leading remote and virtual teams. By leveraging technology, fostering a culture of collaboration, and prioritizing clear and transparent communication, I can overcome the challenges of remote leadership and lead my team to continued success.

Conclusion

As we conclude this chapter on leadership communication, it's important to reflect on the key concepts we've explored and their significance in effective leadership.

Throughout this chapter, we've examined communication's fundamental role in leadership. We discussed essential communication skills such as active listening, empathy, and clarity, highlighting how these skills contribute to effective leadership. Additionally, we explored communication strategies for success, including goal setting, motivation, and conflict resolution, recognizing their importance in driving team performance and achieving organizational goals.

We also delved into the challenges of communication in leadership, acknowledging the complexities of leading remote teams and navigating change and uncertainty. By identifying common communication challenges and discussing strategies for overcoming them, we gained valuable insights into maintaining effectiveness as a leader.

As we look ahead, it's clear that effective communication will continue to be a cornerstone of leadership success. In the next section, we will focus on applying communication strategies for personal and professional growth, exploring how effective communication can drive success in various aspects of life and business.

By embracing the principles and practices of effective communication, we can cultivate strong leadership skills, build meaningful relationships, and achieve our personal and professional goals.

6

APPLYING COMMUNICATION STRATEGIES FOR PERSONAL AND PROFESSIONAL GROWTH

When we talk about personal and professional growth, we're referring to the process of improving oneself both in personal aspects of life and in the professional arena. It's about becoming better versions of ourselves, whether that means enhancing our skills, expanding our knowledge, or achieving our goals.

Effective communication plays a crucial role in this journey of growth. It serves as the foundation upon which we build relationships, collaborate with others, and convey our ideas and aspirations. Without clear and impactful communication, connecting with others, understanding their perspectives, or conveying our thoughts effectively becomes challenging.

In both personal and professional settings, communication acts as a bridge that connects us with growth opportunities. It enables us to seek feedback, learn from experiences, and navigate challenges more effectively. Whether it's expressing our ambitions in a job interview, resolving conflicts with coworkers, or articulating our personal values and beliefs, communication is the key that unlocks the door to our development.

Throughout this chapter, we'll explore how harnessing the power of communication can propel us forward in our journey of personal and professional growth. We'll delve into strategies for enhancing our communication skills, leveraging them to achieve our goals, and ultimately becoming the best versions of ourselves.

COMMUNICATION STRATEGIES FOR PERSONAL GROWTH

Understanding ourselves is the cornerstone of personal growth, and communication is no exception. It begins with self-awareness, which involves recognizing our own communication style and preferences.

For instance, I might discover that I tend to communicate more directly, preferring clear and concise messages over lengthy explanations. Or I might realize that I thrive in one-on-one conversations rather than in group settings. By acknowledging these preferences, I can better tailor my communication approach to suit different situations and audiences.

Self-reflection goes hand in hand with self-awareness. It's about taking the time to examine our interactions and assess their effectiveness. Maybe I notice that I tend to interrupt others during discussions, hindering open dialogue. Or I might recognize that I struggle to convey my thoughts clearly when under pressure. These insights allow me to pinpoint areas for improvement and take proactive steps to enhance my communication skills.

I lay the groundwork for personal growth by investing in self-awareness and self-reflection. Armed with a deeper understanding of myself and my communication tendencies, I can embark on a journey of continuous improvement, striving to become a more effective communicator each day.

Goal setting and action planning are critical steps in my journey toward improving my communication skills. When setting communication goals, I follow the SMART criteria, ensuring they are Specific, Measurable, Achievable, Relevant, and Time-bound.

Let me explain how I approach this. First, I make sure my goals are specific. Instead of setting a vague goal like "improve communication," I define exactly what aspect of communication I want to work on. For example, I might set a goal to improve my public speaking skills by delivering a presentation without using filler words like "um" or "uh."

Next, I ensure my goals are measurable. This means I can track my progress and know when I've achieved them. For instance, I might set a goal to reduce the number of filler words I use in presentations from ten to two per minute.

Achievability is another key consideration. I set goals that are challenging yet realistic. It's important to push myself beyond my comfort zone but not to the point where the goal becomes unattainable. For example, if I'm uncomfortable speaking in front of large groups, I might set a goal to deliver a presentation to a small team before tackling a larger audience.

Relevance is crucial because my goals should align with my overall objectives and priorities. If improving my public speaking skills will help me advance in my career or achieve personal growth, then it's a relevant goal for me.

Finally, I ensure my goals are time-bound by setting deadlines for completion. This adds a sense of urgency and keeps me focused on making progress. For example, I might set a goal to deliver my first filler-word-free presentation within two months.

Once I've set SMART goals, I develop action plans to achieve them. This involves breaking down each goal into smaller, actionable steps. For instance, to reduce filler words in my presentations, I might practice speaking in front of a mirror, record myself to identify patterns, and seek feedback from colleagues.

By setting SMART goals and creating detailed action plans, I give myself a roadmap for success in improving my communication skills. This structured approach helps me stay focused, motivated, and accountable as I work toward becoming a more effective communicator.

Building confidence and assertiveness in communication has been a significant focus for me. One of the first challenges I encountered was overcoming communication apprehension. This apprehension often stemmed from fear of judgment or rejection, which could hinder my ability to express myself effectively.

To overcome this challenge, I took proactive steps to build my confidence. I started by practicing communication in low-stakes situations, such as casual conversations with friends or colleagues. This helped me gradually become more comfortable expressing myself and sharing my thoughts and ideas.

Additionally, I worked on reframing negative thoughts and beliefs about communication. Instead of dwelling on potential mistakes or criticism, I reminded myself that communication is a skill that can be developed over time. By adopting a growth mindset, I became more resilient in the face of challenges and setbacks.

Assertive communication played a crucial role in boosting my confidence. Rather than being passive or aggressive in my communication style, I learned to assertively express my thoughts, feelings, and opinions while respecting the rights of others. This meant speaking up for myself when necessary, setting boundaries, and advocating for my needs in a respectful and diplomatic manner.

I found several techniques helpful for developing assertive communication skills. One technique involved using "I" statements to express my thoughts and feelings without blaming or accusing others. For example, instead of saying, "You never listen to me," I would say, "I feel frustrated when I don't feel heard."

Another technique was practicing active listening, which involved fully engaging with others' perspectives and validating their experiences. By showing empathy and understanding, I could build rapport and strengthen my relationships while asserting my own needs and boundaries.

Through consistent practice and reflection, I gradually became more confident and assertive in my communication style. This newfound confidence improved my interactions with others and empowered me to navigate challenging situations with greater ease and effectiveness.

COMMUNICATION STRATEGIES FOR PROFESSIONAL GROWTH

Networking and relationship building have been instrumental in my professional growth journey. Recognizing the importance of expanding my professional network, I actively sought opportunities to connect with colleagues, industry peers, and potential mentors.

I understood that networking goes beyond simply exchanging business cards or LinkedIn connections. It's about building genuine relationships based on mutual trust and respect. To achieve this, I approached networking with a genuine interest in getting to know others and learning from their experiences.

One strategy I found effective was attending industry events, conferences, and networking mixers. These events provided valuable opportunities to meet like-minded professionals, exchange ideas, and establish meaningful connections. I made a point to engage in conversations, ask questions, and actively listen to others' perspectives.

In addition to in-person networking, I also utilized online platforms such as LinkedIn to expand my professional network. I personalized connection requests and followed up with personalized messages to nurture relationships. Building a strong online presence and sharing relevant content also helped me stay visible and establish credibility within my industry.

Furthermore, I sought out mentorship opportunities to learn from experienced professionals and gain insights into career advancement. I approached potential mentors with humility and a willingness to learn, demonstrating my commitment to personal and professional growth.

Networking and relationship building have been essential to my professional growth strategy. By fostering genuine connections and nurturing relationships, I've been able to expand my network, gain valuable insights, and create opportunities for career advancement.

Developing strong leadership communication skills has been crucial to my journey as a business owner. As I've navigated various leadership roles, I've realized the importance of establishing a strong presence and influence among my team members.

One key aspect of leadership communication is developing a commanding presence that inspires confidence and trust in others. This involves projecting confidence, maintaining a positive demeanor, and demonstrating authenticity in my interactions. By embodying these qualities, I've established myself as a credible and trustworthy leader whom others look up to for guidance and direction.

In addition to presence, effectively communicating vision, goals, and expectations is essential for aligning team members and driving collective efforts toward common objectives. I've learned to articulate my vision in a clear and compelling manner, ensuring that everyone understands the overarching goals and their roles in achieving them. By providing clarity and direction, I've been able to foster a sense of purpose and motivation among my team members, driving them to perform at their best.

Moreover, effective leadership communication involves active listening and empathy, allowing me to understand the needs and concerns of my team members and address them accordingly. By creating an open and supportive communication environment, I've cultivated trust and collaboration within my team, empowering individuals to voice their ideas and contribute to the collective success.

Overall, mastering leadership communication skills has been instrumental in my ability to lead with confidence, inspire others, and achieve collective goals. By continually refining these skills and adapting them to various leadership situations, I've been able to create a positive and impactful leadership presence within my organization.

Negotiation and conflict resolution are vital skills for any business owner. Throughout my career, I've encountered numerous situations where effective negotiation and conflict resolution have been instrumental in achieving favorable outcomes for both myself and my team.

First and foremost, mastering negotiation skills has enabled me to navigate various business scenarios with confidence and finesse. Whether negotiating contracts with suppliers, discussing terms with clients, or resolving disputes internally, having a solid grasp of negotiation principles has allowed me to advocate for my interests while fostering mutually beneficial agreements. By understanding the needs and motivations of all parties involved, I've been able to leverage persuasive communication and problem-solving techniques to reach favorable outcomes.

Similarly, conflict resolution skills have been essential for maintaining harmony and productivity within my organization. In any workplace, conflicts are inevitable, but how they're addressed can make all the difference. By employing effective conflict resolution strategies, such as active listening, empathy, and collaborative problem-solving, I've defused tense situations and facilitated constructive dialogue among team members. By addressing underlying issues and finding win-win solutions, conflicts have often served as opportunities for growth and improvement rather than sources of discord.

Overall, honing negotiation and conflict resolution skills has been pivotal in my business-owner journey. By mastering these essential competencies, I've navigated complex business dynamics with confidence, fostered positive relationships with stakeholders, and drove sustainable growth and success for my organization.

LEVERAGING COMMUNICATION TECHNOLOGY FOR GROWTH

In today's fast-paced business environment, leveraging communication technology is essential for driving growth and staying competitive. Throughout my experience as a business owner, I've learned the importance of harnessing the power of communication tools and platforms to maximize productivity and efficiency.

First and foremost, understanding the landscape of communication tools and platforms is crucial. From email and instant messaging to video conferencing and project management software, many options are available to facilitate communication and collaboration within teams. By familiarizing myself with these tools and their functionalities, I've been able to choose the ones that best align with my business needs and objectives.

Once armed with the right tools, the key is to maximize productivity and efficiency. This involves more than just knowing how to use the technology—it's about integrating it seamlessly into daily workflows. For instance, I've implemented practices such as setting clear communication protocols, establishing designated channels for different types of communication, and leveraging project management software to streamline tasks and deadlines. By optimizing how my team communicates and collaborates, we've accomplished more in less time and driven continuous growth and innovation.

Ultimately, leveraging communication technology isn't just about adopting the latest tools—it's about leveraging them strategically to enhance productivity, efficiency, and, ultimately, business growth. By staying informed about emerging technologies and trends, adapting to the evolving needs of my business, and fostering a culture of innovation and agility, I've been able to harness the full potential of communication technology to propel my business forward.

Ethics and Professionalism in Communication

Ethics and professionalism are foundational pillars of effective communication in both personal and professional settings. As a business owner, I've come to recognize ethical communication's critical role in fostering trust, maintaining integrity, and driving growth.

Ethical communication is more than just following rules and regulations—it's about upholding honesty, transparency, and respect in all interactions. Whether communicating with clients, employees, or stakeholders, I prioritize integrity and strive to ensure that my actions align with ethical standards.

This commitment to ethical communication strengthens relationships and enhances my credibility and reputation as a business leader.

Similarly, professionalism is paramount in every communication interaction. Maintaining professionalism demonstrates competence, reliability, and respect for others, whether it's a formal presentation, an email exchange, or a casual conversation. By adhering to professional standards such as clarity, courtesy, and timeliness, I set a positive example for my team and create an environment conducive to collaboration and success.

Despite our best efforts, navigating ethical dilemmas is inevitable in both personal and professional contexts. Whether it's a conflict of interest, a breach of confidentiality, or a moral dilemma, it's essential to approach these situations with integrity and sensitivity. By considering the perspectives of all parties involved, seeking guidance from mentors or ethical advisors, and making decisions guided by core values, I've navigated ethical challenges with confidence and integrity.

In conclusion, ethics and professionalism are integral communication aspects underpinning personal and professional growth. By prioritizing ethical communication, upholding professionalism, and navigating ethical dilemmas with integrity, I've built strong relationships, earned trust, and driven success in my business endeavors.

Conclusion

As I wrap up this chapter on personal and professional growth through communication, I find myself reflecting on the key concepts that have emerged. Throughout our journey, we've explored the importance of self-awareness, goal-setting, and building confidence in communication. We've also delved into the significance of networking, leadership skills, and ethical communication practices.

Communication isn't just about exchanging words; it's about connecting with others, building relationships, and achieving goals. In both personal and professional contexts, effective communication serves as a catalyst for growth, enabling us to articulate our thoughts, express our ideas, and collaborate with others.

Looking back, I'm reminded of the transformative power of communication in my own journey. By honing my communication skills, setting clear goals, and nurturing relationships, I've been able to overcome challenges, seize opportunities, and chart a path to success.

As we move forward, I'm excited to explore advanced communication strategies for leadership and influence. In the next section, we'll delve deeper into the intricacies of leadership communication, examining how effective communication can inspire others, drive change, and propel organizations toward their goals.

7

ADVANCED COMMUNICATION STRATEGIES FOR LEADERSHIP AND INFLUENCE

As I step into the realm of advanced communication strategies for leadership and influence, I find myself facing an array of powerful tools and techniques. Advanced communication isn't just about conveying messages—it's about shaping perceptions, inspiring action, and leading with influence.

When discussing advanced communication strategies, we're delving into a more nuanced approach to conveying ideas and exerting influence. It's about going beyond the basics of effective communication and tapping into the subtleties that can truly make a difference in how we lead and influence others.

Effective communication lies at the heart of leadership and influence. Whether we're rallying a team around a shared vision, negotiating a deal, or inspiring change, our ability to communicate effectively can make or break our success. In today's fast-paced and interconnected world, where information is constantly flowing and attention spans are fleeting, mastering advanced communication strategies is more critical than ever before.

In this chapter, we'll explore the definition of advanced communication strategies and their pivotal role in leadership and influence. We'll uncover the intricacies of these strategies and how they can be wielded to achieve our goals and drive meaningful outcomes. So, let's dive in and uncover the secrets to mastering advanced communication in the realm of leadership and influence.

Harnessing the Power of Persuasion

As I delve into the realm of persuasion, I'm struck by its immense power in shaping perceptions and driving action. Understanding the principles that underpin persuasion is like unlocking a hidden treasure trove of influence—one that can profoundly impact how we lead and communicate.

At its core, persuasion operates on principles that tap into fundamental aspects of human psychology. These principles, such as reciprocity, authority, consistency, social proof, liking, and scarcity, are the building blocks of persuasive communication.

Reciprocity is the idea that we feel compelled to give something in return when we receive something. It's like an instinct that drives us to reciprocate kindness or favors.

Authority plays on our tendency to defer to those we perceive as knowledgeable or credible. Whether it's a doctor giving medical advice or a CEO outlining a strategic vision, authority figures hold sway over our decisions.

Consistency is about our desire to align our actions with our beliefs and commitments. Once we've made a public commitment or taken a stand on something, we're more likely to stick to it to maintain consistency.

Social proof leverages the power of social influence, showing that people are more likely to adopt a behavior if they see others doing it. It's why testimonials, endorsements, and peer recommendations carry so much weight in persuading us.

Liking is based on the principle that we're more easily persuaded by people we know, like, and trust. Building rapport and fostering connections can significantly enhance our ability to persuade others.

Scarcity taps into our fear of missing out, highlighting the limited availability of something to spur action. Whether it's a limited-time offer or exclusive access, scarcity drives us to act before it's too late.

Reflecting on these principles, I realize their profound implications for leadership communication. Crafting compelling narratives that resonate with our audience and using rhetorical devices to drive home our message can amplify the persuasive impact of our communication.

In essence, harnessing the power of persuasion isn't just about convincing others—it's about building trust, inspiring action, and leading with influence. By mastering these principles and applying them skillfully in our communication, we can unlock new levels of effectiveness as leaders.

BUILDING A PERSONAL BRAND THROUGH COMMUNICATION

As I reflect on personal branding, I realize its profound impact on how others perceive me and my business. It's not just about having a logo or a catchy tagline—it's about crafting a compelling narrative that showcases who I am and what I stand for.

Personal branding is like painting a picture of myself in the minds of others. It's about defining what sets me apart from the crowd and communicating that in a way that resonates with my audience.

One of the key strategies for building a strong personal brand is defining my unique value proposition. What do I bring to the table that others don't? Whether it's my expertise, passion, or approach to solving problems, clarifying my unique value proposition helps me stand out in a crowded marketplace.

Consistency is another crucial aspect of personal branding. Every touchpoint is an opportunity to reinforce my brand identity, from my website to my social media profiles to my interactions with clients. Consistency breeds familiarity, and familiarity breeds trust.

But perhaps the most powerful tool in my personal branding arsenal is storytelling. Storytelling has a way of capturing attention, evoking emotions, and making a lasting impression. I can create a powerful connection with my audience by weaving my personal experiences, successes, and values into compelling narratives.

As I embark on this journey of building my personal brand, I'm excited to see how it shapes how others perceive me and how I see myself. It's not just about creating a brand—it's about crafting a legacy that reflects who I am and what I aspire to be. And through strategic communication, I know I can bring that vision to life.

STRATEGIC COMMUNICATION FOR ORGANIZATIONAL CHANGE

Navigating organizational change is like steering a ship through stormy waters—it requires clear direction, effective communication, and the ability to rally everyone on board toward a common goal.

Communication plays a pivotal role in change management. It's not just about disseminating information; it's about inspiring confidence, fostering understanding, and encouraging buy-in from all levels of the organization.

Creating a sense of urgency is one of the first steps in implementing successful change. Without a compelling reason to change, people are likely to resist. By articulating the need for change and highlighting the consequences of maintaining the status quo, I can galvanize support and create momentum for the change initiative.

Engaging stakeholders is another critical aspect of effective change communication. Whether it's frontline employees, middle managers, or senior executives, everyone has a role to play in the change process. I can foster a sense of ownership and commitment to the change effort by soliciting feedback, addressing concerns, and involving stakeholders in decision-making.

Transparency is also paramount in change communication. People crave honesty and authenticity, especially during times of uncertainty. By providing clear, timely, and transparent communication about the change initiative's what, why, and how, I can mitigate rumors, alleviate fears, and build trust among employees.

As I embark on this journey of organizational change, I'm mindful of the importance of strategic communication. By leveraging communication as a powerful tool for driving change, I can confidently and clearly navigate the choppy waters of organizational transformation. By keeping my crew informed, engaged, and motivated every step of the way, I know we can weather any storm that comes our way.

INFLUENCING ACROSS HIERARCHIES AND TEAMS

In the complex ecosystem of organizations, navigating hierarchies and influencing across teams requires finesse and strategic communication. As a business owner, I've learned that breaking down communication barriers in hierarchical structures is essential for fostering collaboration and driving results.

In hierarchical organizations, communication can sometimes get bogged down as it moves up and down the chain of command. As a leader, I recognize the importance of breaking through these barriers to ensure that information flows freely and everyone feels heard and valued.

One strategy for influencing peers and superiors is to build alliances and coalitions. By cultivating relationships with key stakeholders across different levels of the organization, I can garner support for my ideas and initiatives. These alliances give me the credibility and backing needed to enact change and drive progress.

Another powerful tool for influencing across hierarchies is leveraging social capital. This involves tapping into the informal networks and relationships that exist within the organization. By cultivating a strong personal brand, demonstrating expertise, and fostering trust and respect among my peers and superiors, I can effectively leverage my social capital to influence decision-making and drive alignment toward common goals.

Also, fostering collaboration and teamwork through effective communication is essential for success in any organization. By promoting open dialogue, encouraging the sharing of ideas and perspectives, and facilitating constructive feedback, I can create an environment where teams feel empowered to collaborate, innovate, and achieve collective goals.

Ultimately, by overcoming communication barriers, building alliances, and fostering collaboration across hierarchies and teams, I can harness my organization's collective intelligence and capabilities to drive growth, innovation, and success.

CRISIS COMMUNICATION AND REPUTATION MANAGEMENT

In the fast-paced business world, crises can happen unexpectedly and threaten any organization's reputation and stability. As a business owner, I understand the importance of being proactive in crisis communication planning to effectively manage unforeseen challenges.

One of the key strategies for managing communication during a crisis is transparency and honesty. When faced with a crisis, it's crucial to communicate openly and honestly with stakeholders, including employees, customers, and the public. By providing accurate information and acknowledging any mistakes or shortcomings, I can build trust and credibility, which are essential for navigating through challenging times.

Additionally, a swift response and decisive action are critical in crisis management. It's essential to act quickly to address the situation, mitigate any potential damage, and reassure stakeholders that steps are being taken to resolve the issue. By demonstrating leadership and taking decisive action, I can instill confidence in my organization's ability to weather the storm and emerge stronger on the other side.

In the aftermath of a crisis, rebuilding trust and reputation becomes paramount. This involves addressing the immediate issues and implementing long-term strategies to repair any damage to the organization's reputation. I can gradually rebuild trust and credibility with stakeholders by being transparent about lessons learned, making meaningful changes, and consistently delivering on promises.

Overall, I can effectively navigate challenging times and emerge stronger as a business leader by proactively planning for crises, communicating transparently and honestly, taking swift and decisive action, and focusing on rebuilding trust and reputation.

LEVERAGING DIGITAL PLATFORMS FOR INFLUENCE

In today's digital age, leveraging digital platforms is essential for any business looking to expand its influence and reach. As a business owner, I understand the importance of effectively utilizing digital communication channels to connect with my audience and build influence.

Digital communication channels encompass various platforms, including social media, websites, blogs, email, and more. Each platform offers unique opportunities to engage with audiences and share valuable content.

One key strategy for building influence through social media is content creation and curation. By consistently sharing relevant and engaging content, I can establish myself as a thought leader in my industry and attract a loyal following. Whether it's sharing industry insights, showcasing products or services, or providing helpful tips and advice, valuable content helps to establish credibility and build trust with my audience.

Engaging with online communities is another effective strategy for building influence on digital platforms. By actively participating in relevant online communities and discussions, I can connect with like-minded individuals, share valuable insights, and build relationships with potential customers or clients. Engaging with my audience meaningfully helps foster trust and loyalty, ultimately enhancing my influence within the digital space.

Digital storytelling is a powerful tool for capturing my audience's attention and conveying my brand's message effectively. By sharing compelling stories through various digital channels, such as videos, blog posts, or social media posts, I can create an emotional connection with my audience and showcase the human side of my brand. Whether it's sharing customer success stories, behind-the-scenes glimpses of my business, or personal anecdotes, storytelling helps humanize my brand and make it more relatable.

In conclusion, leveraging digital platforms for influence involves creating and sharing valuable content, engaging with online communities, and harnessing the power of digital storytelling. By effectively utilizing these strategies, I can expand my influence, reach a wider audience, and ultimately achieve my business goals in the digital landscape.

COMMUNICATION ETHICS IN LEADERSHIP AND INFLUENCE

As a business owner, I recognize the critical importance of upholding ethical communication practices in all aspects of leadership and influence. Ethical communication forms the foundation of trust, credibility, and integrity in my interactions with others.

Ethical communication involves being truthful, transparent, and respectful in my communication with stakeholders, colleagues, and customers. By prioritizing honesty and integrity in my communication practices, I can build trust and foster positive relationships with those around me.

When it comes to persuasion and influence, ethical considerations are paramount. While it may be tempting to use persuasive tactics to achieve my desired outcomes, ensuring that my communication remains ethical and respectful of others' autonomy and rights is essential. This means avoiding manipulation, coercion, or deception in my persuasive efforts and instead focusing on providing accurate information and allowing individuals to make informed decisions.

Navigating ethical dilemmas in leadership communication requires careful consideration and ethical judgment. As a leader, I may encounter situations where ethical principles come into conflict, requiring me to make difficult decisions. In such instances, I must prioritize ethical values and principles, even if it means facing challenges or setbacks in the short term. By upholding ethical standards in my leadership communication, I can maintain my integrity and credibility as a leader and inspire trust and confidence in those I lead.

In conclusion, communication ethics play a vital role in leadership and influence. By prioritizing ethical communication practices, considering ethical considerations in persuasion and influence, and navigating ethical dilemmas with integrity and judgment, I can demonstrate my commitment to ethical leadership and build positive relationships with others.

Conclusion

In wrapping up this chapter, I've gained valuable insights into advanced communication strategies for leadership and influence. We've covered a lot of ground, from the principles of persuasion to crisis communication and the ethical considerations that underpin effective leadership communication.

Looking back, I realize just how crucial it is to master these advanced communication techniques. Whether it's crafting persuasive narratives, navigating organizational change, or leveraging digital platforms for influence, these strategies can truly make a difference in how I lead and inspire others.

As I reflect on the importance of these concepts, I'm reminded that communication lies at the heart of effective leadership. By honing my communication skills and embracing advanced strategies, I can better connect with my team, influence stakeholders, and drive positive change within my organization.

Our journey doesn't end here. In the next section, we'll shift our focus to the future of communication in business. From emerging technologies to evolving consumer preferences, we'll explore how communication continues to shape the way we do business in a rapidly changing world. So, let's stay tuned and keep evolving with the times.

8

THE FUTURE OF COMMUNICATION IN BUSINESS

As a business owner, staying ahead of the curve in communication is essential. That's why I'm diving into the future of communication in business. It's not just about sending emails or making phone calls anymore. Communication technology and trends are evolving rapidly, and understanding and adapting to these changes is crucial for success.

When we talk about the future of communication in business, we're referring to how we connect and interact with customers, employees, and stakeholders. It's about leveraging new technologies, embracing shifting preferences, and staying ahead of the curve in a fast-paced digital world.

The significance of this topic cannot be overstated. As communication methods evolve, so do customer expectations. Businesses that fail to adapt risk falling behind the competition. By understanding and embracing the future of communication, we can stay relevant, engage our audience effectively, and drive business growth.

Emerging Communication
Technologies

In the ever-evolving landscape of business communication, keeping up with emerging technologies is crucial. That's why I'm diving into the realm of AI, VR, AR, and IoT – these aren't just buzzwords; they're shaping the future of how we connect and engage with our audience.

Artificial Intelligence (AI) is revolutionizing how businesses interact with customers. From chatbots that provide instant support to predictive analytics that personalize marketing campaigns, AI is streamlining processes and enhancing customer experiences.

Virtual Reality (VR) and Augmented Reality (AR) are no longer just for gaming. Businesses are leveraging these immersive technologies for training simulations, virtual product demos, and even virtual meetings, breaking down geographical barriers and offering unique experiences.

The Internet of Things (IoT) is connecting devices like never before, enabling seamless communication between objects and systems. From smart home devices to industrial sensors, IoT is optimizing processes, improving efficiency, and creating new opportunities for businesses to interact with customers.

The implications of these technologies for business communication are vast. They allow for more personalized and interactive experiences, increased efficiency and automation, and a deeper understanding of customer behavior through data analytics.

To illustrate the real-world impact, I'll explore case studies and examples of businesses successfully leveraging these emerging technologies. From startups to multinational corporations, businesses across industries are embracing these tools to stay ahead of the curve and revolutionize the way they communicate.

EVOLUTION OF CUSTOMER COMMUNICATION

In the world of business, understanding how customers want to communicate is essential. Over time, I've noticed shifts in their preferences, and it's crucial to adapt to these changes to stay connected. That's why I'm exploring the evolution of customer communication.

Customers today expect more than just a phone call or an email. They want convenience and flexibility, which has led to a rise in various communication channels. The options are endless, from social media and messaging apps to chatbots and voice assistants. As a business owner, it's essential to meet customers where they are and offer multiple touchpoints for communication.

Omnichannel communication strategies have become increasingly important. This approach ensures a seamless experience across all channels, allowing customers to transition effortlessly from one platform to another without losing context. Whether they're browsing your website, sending a message on social media, or calling your support line, they expect consistency and continuity.

Personalization and customization are also key trends in customer communication. Customers want to feel valued and understood, and generic messages no longer cut it. By leveraging data and technology, businesses can tailor their communication to each individual customer, delivering relevant content and offers that resonate on a personal level.

In my experience, embracing these shifts in customer communication preferences has been crucial for building strong relationships and fostering loyalty. By staying ahead of the curve and providing a seamless, personalized experience, I've been able to connect with customers in meaningful ways and drive business growth.

REMOTE WORK AND DISTRIBUTED TEAMS

In today's fast-paced business landscape, remote work and distributed teams have become increasingly common. This shift has been driven by various factors, including advances in technology, changing attitudes toward work-life balance, and the need for flexibility in a globalized world. As a business owner, I've seen firsthand the rise of remote work and the challenges and opportunities it presents.

One of the most significant benefits of remote work is the ability to access a global talent pool. Instead of being limited to hiring locally, businesses can now recruit top talent from around the world, bringing diverse perspectives and skills to their teams. This flexibility also allows employees to work from anywhere, whether in a coffee shop, co-working space, or home.

However, remote work also comes with its own set of communication challenges. Without face-to-face interaction, building trust, fostering collaboration, and maintaining camaraderie among team members can be more difficult. Miscommunications can occur more easily, leading to delays, misunderstandings, and decreased productivity.

To overcome these challenges, it's essential to implement strategies for effective communication and collaboration in remote teams. This may include setting clear expectations around communication channels and response times, leveraging technology tools such as video conferencing and instant messaging, and establishing regular check-ins to provide feedback and support.

In my own business, I've found that fostering a culture of open communication and transparency is key to success in a remote work environment. By prioritizing clear communication, setting realistic goals, and empowering team members to take ownership of their work, we've overcome the challenges of remote work and achieved our business objectives.

SUSTAINABILITY AND CORPORATE SOCIAL RESPONSIBILITY (CSR) COMMUNICATION

Sustainability and corporate social responsibility (CSR) have become increasingly important in today's business landscape. Customers, investors, and employees are placing greater emphasis on companies that prioritize environmental stewardship, social impact, and ethical business practices. As a business owner, I've recognized the significance of integrating sustainability and CSR into our communication strategies.

Communicating sustainability initiatives effectively requires a thoughtful approach that goes beyond simply sharing information about environmental efforts. It involves storytelling, transparency, and engagement to effectively convey the company's values and commitment to positive change. One strategy we've employed is aligning our sustainability goals with our overall business objectives, demonstrating that environmental and social responsibility are integral to our corporate identity.

Case studies of companies leading in sustainability communication provide valuable insights and inspiration for businesses looking to enhance their own efforts. These companies often leverage various communication channels like social media, corporate websites, and annual reports to share their sustainability initiatives with stakeholders. By highlighting tangible outcomes, engaging with stakeholders, and addressing challenges transparently, these companies effectively demonstrate their commitment to sustainability and CSR.

In my own business, we've made sustainability and CSR central to our communication strategy. We regularly communicate our sustainability goals, initiatives, and progress through our website, social media channels, and annual reports. We aim to foster trust, build brand loyalty, and create positive social and environmental impact by engaging with our customers, employees, and other stakeholders. As sustainability continues to gain importance in business communication, we remain committed to leading by example and driving meaningful change in our industry.

The Role of Data and Analytics

In today's digital age, data has become a crucial tool for businesses, including mine, to understand customer behavior, track trends, and make informed decisions. As a business owner, I've come to appreciate the importance of data-driven communication strategies in effectively reaching and engaging with our target audience.

By leveraging data and analytics, we can gain valuable insights into our customers' preferences, interests, and purchasing habits. This allows us to tailor our communication efforts to resonate with our audience more personally. For example, by analyzing customer data, we can identify the most effective channels, messaging, and timing for our marketing campaigns, ensuring that we reach the right people with the right message at the right time.

Analytics also play a vital role in optimizing communication effectiveness. By monitoring key performance indicators (KPIs) such as engagement rates, conversion rates, and customer satisfaction scores, we can evaluate the success of our communication initiatives and make data-driven adjustments to improve results over time. For instance, if we notice a decline in email open rates, we can experiment with different subject lines or content formats to see what resonates best with our audience.

However, it's essential to approach data usage for communication with integrity and respect for privacy. Ethical considerations become increasingly important as businesses collect and analyze vast amounts of data. We must be transparent about how we collect, store, and use data and ensure that we comply with relevant regulations, such as GDPR or CCPA. Respecting customers' privacy and maintaining their trust is paramount in today's data-driven business environment.

In my own business, we prioritize ethical data practices and transparency in our communication efforts. We take great care to protect customer data and only use it in ways that benefit our customers and align with their expectations. By harnessing the power of data responsibly, we can continue to enhance our communication strategies and deliver value to our customers while maintaining their trust and confidence in our brand.

Adaptation to Changing Regulatory Landscape

As a business owner, staying on top of changing regulations is vital to ensuring that my communication practices are effective and compliant with the law. Over the years, there have been significant developments in regulations that govern how businesses can communicate with their customers, such as GDPR (General Data Protection Regulation) and CCPA (California Consumer Privacy Act).

These regulations aim to protect consumers' privacy and give them more control over how businesses collect, use, and share their personal data. While navigating these regulatory landscapes can be challenging, it's essential to prioritize compliance to maintain trust and credibility with our customers.

One of the key strategies we employ to ensure compliance is to stay informed about the latest regulatory updates and seek legal advice when needed. By understanding the requirements of regulations like GDPR and CCPA, we can implement appropriate measures to protect customer data and ensure that our communication practices align with legal standards.

For example, GDPR requires businesses to obtain explicit consent from individuals before collecting their personal data and to provide clear and transparent information about how that data will be used. In response to this requirement, we have updated our privacy policies and implemented procedures to obtain customer consent when necessary.

In addition to legal compliance, we also recognize the importance of maintaining customer trust. Being transparent about our data practices and respecting their privacy preferences can build stronger relationships with our customers and enhance their confidence in our brand.

Overall, the changing regulatory landscape presents both challenges and opportunities for businesses. While compliance may require adjustments to communication practices, it also provides an opportunity to demonstrate our commitment to protecting customer privacy and maintaining ethical standards in our business operations. By proactively adapting to these changes, we can continue communicating effectively while building trust and credibility with our customers.

Future Trends and Predictions

As a business owner, keeping an eye on future trends in communication is crucial for staying ahead of the curve and adapting our strategies accordingly. Looking ahead, I anticipate several key trends will shape the landscape of business communication in the coming years.

First and foremost, I expect to see continued advancements in communication technologies. From artificial intelligence (AI) and virtual reality (VR) to augmented reality (AR) and the Internet of Things (IoT), these emerging technologies have the potential to revolutionize how businesses communicate with their customers and stakeholders. For example, AI-powered chatbots can provide personalized customer support around the clock, while VR and AR technologies can enhance remote collaboration and training experiences.

Another trend I foresee is the growing emphasis on interactive and immersive communication experiences. As consumers become more accustomed to interactive content, businesses must find creative ways to engage their audiences and capture their attention. This could involve leveraging interactive videos, live streaming, and gamification techniques to create more memorable and engaging communication experiences.

Furthermore, I believe there will be a greater focus on sustainability and ethical communication practices. With increasing awareness of environmental and social issues, consumers are becoming more discerning about the companies they support and the values they espouse. Businesses prioritizing transparency, authenticity, and corporate social responsibility (CSR) in their communication efforts will likely resonate more with their audience and build stronger brand loyalty.

Regarding implications for businesses and professionals, staying agile and adaptable will be key. As communication technologies and consumer preferences evolve, businesses must proactively embrace change and experiment with new strategies. This may involve investing in employee training and development to ensure that our teams have the skills and knowledge needed to navigate the changing landscape of business communication effectively.

Overall, while the future of communication in business is uncertain, by staying informed, remaining open to innovation, and prioritizing ethical and sustainable practices, we can position ourselves for success in the years to come.

Conclusion

In wrapping up this chapter, I've gained valuable insights into the future of communication in business. We've explored emerging technologies, evolving customer preferences, and the shifting regulatory landscape, which will shape how we communicate with our audiences in the years ahead.

One key takeaway is the importance of adaptability. As communication technologies continue to evolve and consumer behaviors change, businesses must remain flexible and open to new approaches. Whether embracing AI-powered chatbots to enhance customer service or leveraging interactive content to engage our audience, being willing to adapt will be critical for staying competitive in the marketplace.

Furthermore, I've been reminded of the significance of ethical and transparent communication practices. As consumers become more discerning about the companies they support, maintaining trust and credibility through ethical communication will be essential for building long-term relationships with our customers and stakeholders.

As we look to the future, I'm encouraged by the opportunities that lie ahead. We can position ourselves for success in an ever-changing business landscape by staying proactive and innovative in our communication approaches. I urge fellow business owners to join me in this endeavor, embracing change and seizing opportunities to connect with our audiences in meaningful and impactful ways. Together, we can navigate the future of communication in business with confidence and resilience.

CONCLUSION: MAXIMIZING BUSINESS EFFICIENCY AND CUSTOMER SATISFACTION

Throughout my exploration of maximizing business efficiency and customer satisfaction, one of the fundamental lessons that resonated deeply is efficient communication's pivotal role. This isn't just about talking well; it's about how every aspect of communication, from emails to team meetings, influences our ability to succeed.

Effective communication isn't just a tool; it's the bedrock upon which businesses thrive. It ensures clarity in instructions, alignment in goals, and, ultimately, customer satisfaction. By honing our communication skills internally within our teams and externally with our clients, we create an environment where productivity and customer loyalty flourish.

Strategically, I've learned that fostering an open and clear communication culture isn't just a nice-to-have; it's a strategic imperative. From utilizing the right digital tools for seamless collaboration to implementing feedback loops that ensure everyone is heard, each strategy discussed in the book underscores the importance of proactive communication.

Looking ahead, I'm inspired to apply these insights within my own business. By prioritizing efficient communication, I aim to streamline operations, boost employee morale, and deliver exceptional service that delights our customers. These lessons have equipped me with practical strategies and reinforced the transformative power of clear and effective communication in driving business success.

As I reflect on the actionable tips and strategies discussed in this book, I'm struck by how practical and transformative they can be for any business aiming to maximize efficiency through improved communication.

Firstly, the exploration of communication tools and technologies was eye-opening. From project management software that streamlines collaboration to video conferencing platforms that bridge geographical gaps, these tools are not just about convenience—they're essential for modern business operations. Implementing these technologies can significantly enhance productivity by facilitating faster decision-making and smoother workflows.

Equally important were the best practices for fostering a communicative culture within teams. It's not just about having the right tools; it's about creating an environment where communication thrives. This means encouraging open dialogue, active listening, and constructive feedback among team members. By nurturing a culture where everyone feels heard and valued, we can foster innovation, boost morale, and achieve better outcomes for our clients.

I'm eager to integrate these insights into my business practices. By adopting effective communication tools and cultivating a communicative culture, I believe we can enhance teamwork, minimize misunderstandings, and deliver superior customer service. These strategies are not just theoretical but practical steps that can make a tangible difference in how we operate and succeed in a competitive business landscape.

Reflecting on the transformative power of effective communication in business highlights how foundational it is for success. Throughout this journey of understanding, I've come to appreciate the immediate impacts and the profound long-term benefits it can bring to any organization.

Improved communication isn't just about clearer emails or more effective meetings; it's about gaining a competitive edge in a crowded marketplace. When teams communicate well, projects move faster, decisions are more informed, and customer needs are better understood and met. This translates directly into better outcomes for our clients and ultimately positions us ahead of competitors who may struggle with communication bottlenecks.

Beyond immediate gains, fostering a culture of effective communication has lasting impacts on organizational culture and employee morale. When communication flows freely and transparently, it builds trust among team members. Employees feel valued and empowered, leading to higher job satisfaction and lower turnover rates. This positive culture becomes a magnet for talent and enhances our reputation as an employer of choice in the industry.

Leadership plays a pivotal role in shaping this communicative environment. By setting clear communication goals and expectations, leaders provide a roadmap for their teams. When leaders model these behaviors themselves—being open to feedback, listening actively, and communicating with empathy—it sets a standard that others follow. This leadership enhances day-to-day operations and cultivates a collaborative atmosphere where innovation thrives.

Looking ahead, the future of business communication is exciting yet challenging. Emerging technologies like artificial intelligence and virtual reality are poised to revolutionize our collaboration and communication. These innovations will likely streamline processes, enhance remote work capabilities, and open new avenues for global connectivity. As these trends evolve, businesses that embrace and adapt to these technologies will maintain their competitive edge in a rapidly changing landscape.

By continually investing in our communication strategies, embracing new technologies, and nurturing a culture of openness and collaboration, we ensure our current success and our readiness for future opportunities and challenges in the dynamic business world.

Implementing effective communication strategies isn't just about adopting new tools or holding occasional workshops—it's about embedding these practices into the daily fabric of our business operations.

One of the most practical steps we've found is investing in comprehensive training programs that focus on enhancing communication skills across our team. These programs aren't just about basic communication etiquette; they delve into active listening, clarity in messaging, and adapting communication styles to different audiences. We're laying a strong foundation for effective teamwork and client interactions by equipping our employees with these skills.

Alongside training, implementing efficient communication channels is crucial. This involves selecting and integrating tools and resources that facilitate seamless communication. From project management platforms that centralize discussions and updates to instant messaging apps that enable quick queries and updates, these tools streamline workflows and reduce misunderstandings.

Measuring the effectiveness of our communication efforts is equally important. We've established clear metrics and benchmarks to gauge success, such as response times to client inquiries, feedback from team members on clarity of instructions, and customer satisfaction ratings related to communication. These metrics help us identify areas needing improvement and celebrate successes where communication has excelled.

Continuous improvement is a guiding principle in refining our communication practices. We regularly review feedback from both internal stakeholders and clients to identify patterns or recurring challenges. This iterative process allows us to adapt and evolve our communication strategies in response to changing business needs and technological advancements.

In wrapping up our discussion on communication in business, I want to leave you with a clear call to action—an invitation to take proactive steps that can truly transform how your organization operates.

First and foremost, I encourage you to prioritize communication as a strategic initiative within your business. It's not just about sending messages or holding meetings; it's about fostering a culture where every interaction, whether internal or external, is clear, effective, and purposeful. When communication flows smoothly, it enhances productivity, reduces errors, and builds stronger relationships with your team and customers.

I invite you to reflect on the insights and strategies shared here and consider how they can be tailored to fit your specific organizational needs. Communication isn't a one-size-fits-all approach, so feel empowered to adapt these principles to suit your company's unique culture and challenges.

As you embark on this journey, I encourage you to share your experiences and seek feedback from your team. Communication is a collaborative effort, and by listening to different perspectives and learning from both successes and setbacks, you'll continuously refine and improve your approach.

Finally, I want to inspire you to see yourself as a catalyst for positive change through effective communication. Imagine a future where every team member feels heard, ideas flow freely, and challenges are tackled with clarity and purpose. By committing to enhancing communication within your organization, you're not just improving workflows—you're laying the groundwork for sustained growth and success.

Together, let's envision and work toward a future where efficient communication is not just a tool but a cornerstone of business excellence. Let's empower each other to embrace communication as a powerful driver of innovation, collaboration, and overall business success. The journey starts with each of us taking deliberate steps to communicate better and build a stronger, more cohesive team.

Work Less and Make More Money Than Ever Before

Take your business to the next level
with a fresh perspective.

Jason Miller's insights show you exactly how to break
through plateaus and achieve big profits.

Go beyond your expectations and
see what's possible for your business.

jetlaunch.link/SABdiscover

About the Author

Jason Miller is an accomplished business leader with over thirty years of experience, renowned for his expertise in hyper company growth, scaling, and strategic and operational implementation. He founded the Strategic Advisor Board (SAB) in 2017 and served as its Senior Global Council Member, overseeing its global operations and team capabilities. In addition to his primary role at SAB, Jason holds multiple chair positions across various companies and nonprofits. He has built more than twenty-four companies from scratch since 2001 and is dedicated to crafting sustainable business models emphasizing leadership responsibility, strategy, and accountability.

Known for his no-excuses approach and nicknamed "The Bull," Jason has advised thousands of global leaders. He has been recognized as a foremost expert in consulting for creating scalable business models, particularly for small and mid-market companies. His focus extends to fostering a positive company culture, enhancing staff retention, and deepening customer loyalty, believing that a clear vision and purpose are essential for impactful business. As a veteran, Jason is committed to serving veteran-owned companies and provides pro bono services to veteran organizations as part of a five-year plan.

Jason holds an MBA from Trident University and credits the "school of hard knocks" for his doctorate in practical experience. He is affiliated with numerous prestigious organizations that impact business globally, such as the American Club Association, Leigh Steinberg Academy, Forbes Council, and Entrepreneur Magazine Leadership Council. A lifetime member of the American Legion, Disabled American Veterans, and Veterans of Foreign Wars, Jason lives in Boulder, Colorado, with his family. He focuses on professional development and business strategy to serve his clients better.

www.ingramcontent.com/pod-product-compliance
Lightning Source LLC
Chambersburg PA
CBHW050526190326
41458CB00045B/6718/J